Getting High and Doing Time: What's the Connection?

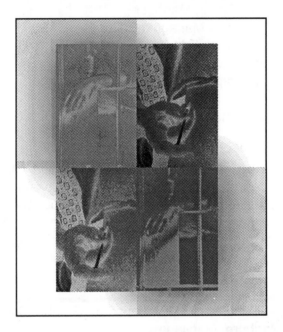

A Recovery Guide for Substance Abusers in Trouble with the Law

Second Edition

**Edward M. Read, LCSW, MAC
and Dennis C. Daley, Ph.D.**

**American Correctional Association
Lanham, Maryland**

Dedication

To James Hedglin, Sr., and Jerome Schneier, in appreciation for influencing me in positive ways. —D.C.D.

To my precious wife, Lee, who by sheer example has shared with me an indispensable secret to sustaining inner peace, one day at a time: learning to want what I need and not needing what I want, and to my equally precious children, Sofia and AJ, without whom I would simply be nothing.—E.M.R.

Table of Contents

Foreword

There are more than five million individuals under some type of supervision in the United States today. According to the Bureau of Justice Statistics, offenders convicted of drug crimes have more than tripled in the past ten years. After release, two-thirds will commit additional crimes to support their addiction, returning for a second or third term of incarceration. Although the figures vary slightly depending on the source, somewhere between 60 and 75 percent of all crimes are in some way related to the use and abuse of alcohol or other drugs.

Many people who become involved in the criminal justice system—prison, jail, probation or some other form of supervision—have a problem with drugs or alcohol, but do not realize it. They do not "make the connection" between their trouble with the law and their substance abuse. This book is designed to help those people—through self-examination—realize their problem and do something about it, either through Alcoholics Anonymous, Narcotics Anonymous, or more formal treatment programs. We hope that this book will help readers start on the road to sobriety, self-enlightenment, and recovery for a life more fulfilling and promising.

James A. Gondles, Jr., CAE
Executive Director
American Correctional Association

Foreword

There are more than five million individuals in the United States today...

Introduction

We Talked "Around" Our Addiction

We are glad you decided to read this book. Try to keep an open mind as you read. Go slowly and think back on your life. See if you can relate to the people mentioned. Listen to Lamont, Alex, Byron, and Judy as they share some of themselves with you. They are composites or combinations of people we have worked with in various programs. They may be like you. And you may learn something from them. It could help turn your life around or even save it.

A bum rap

I'm back in the joint for the third god-damn time! This is such bullshit, man. I'm so tired of this crap. Got locked up bumping off this dude for some cash. I wasn't even smoking nothing at the time, I'd just done some Hennessy and Colt 45 with some friends. No big thing, really. And then, shit, here I am acting crazy and talking shit rolling this guy I know had some extra cash.

Oh yeah, I was thinking about smoking crack by then, I mean after the bumper, but shit, I'd been straight from cocaine for three damn months on my own by then. I just lose it around these guys I been hanging with. I ain't even gonna hook up with them again. This is it.

— Lamont, age 32

The DWI blues

I just came from court. Got two years probation for my second drunk driving arrest. My PO says he wants me to go to AA meetings. He thinks I might be an alcoholic or "problem drinker." I can't believe I let this happen to me again. I can usually handle my drinking. Most of the time I drive home from the clubs because my buddies are too screwed up to drive.

My PO is talking about me showing "signs of alcoholism." Sure, I like my drinks after work and on the weekend, but I'm no alco-

holic. I have a good job with lots of benefits. It's the pressure of the job, my wife's nagging, and all the bills—that's my real problem. Now, my dad was an alcoholic; he drank morning, noon, and night. Always argued with Mom and got fired a lot. Not me. I'm not like him at all. I just have to cut down a bit and be more careful when I drive.

— Alex, age 45

Just a snort or two, one more—I can't stop!

I'm in serious trouble now. My family taught me to obey the law. I had a good education and my family was rich. My life was going very well—until I started snorting heroin. Just a little at first, 'cause it wasn't like I was shooting it, you know. No chance of AIDS; just a nice and warm buzz. I didn't even really like it the first time, but my friends kept bugging me to use with them. And then it was like a switch turned on—I couldn't stop! And that was the beginning of the end. I just couldn't stop, even though God knows I tried and tried. l made a lot of promises to stop.

I spent a lot of money on dope and finally had to start selling it. Can you imagine that? Me selling drugs. Before I knew what hit me, I totally lost control over my actions. I didn't even care. I could not think straight. Well, I finally got arrested a couple of times and sent to prison. I may not be able to make it inside here!

— Byron, age 20

Getting high and going back

I'm on my way back to prison. Yeah, my parole man had me going to this drug program and these Narcotics Anonymous meetings. The MF made me get slips signed. If that ain't nothing, the dude also had me piss in a bottle to make sure I was staying clean from dope. I started coming up dirty so he had me go to more meetings. He started saying I was an "addict" and shit.

Yeah, I went to those NA meetings. What bullshit, talking sobriety and Higher Power shit. What do they know about where I come from? Shit, I got my slips signed by some of my running people. My PO don't care or he don't know the damn difference. He don't know shit anyway 'cause he never been where I am. I'm tired of the crap I gotta put up with. I'm getting too old for this shit.

— Judy, age 27

From Ecstasy to misery

They call 'em "club drugs." You know what I'm talking about, Ecstasy, X, XTC, Special K (Ketamine), Roofies (Rohypnol) or Adam (Ecstasy). I'd been using crystal meth or "crank" for several years, but then I went to this wild "rave" party downtown. Hooked up with Brian and some of his friends who turned me on to these pills, called Ecstasy. Wow, I danced all night long. I couldn't seem to stop. And then it happened—Brian fell out—he'd taken a handful of those suckers. He was  in bad shape and hardly got it together, had to be hospitalized. It scared the shit out of me—that stuff can be really dangerous. I've had it. I'm stopping. The only trouble is, I don't think I can do it alone.

— Sheila, age 18

Have you promised you'd never get locked up? Or have you promised that you would stop using drugs or stop drinking too much before the cops got involved? Or what about the promise that the minute you had to deal with a probation officer, you could get yourself together? That is what all the previous examples had in common. That is just what they thought, too. They did not plan on going to the joint, having a probation officer in their life, or being called an addict or alcoholic. It just came down that way.

What is going on here? Now is the time you may want to ask, "Why?" How could you have let it happen again? Or was it just not your fault or problem at all? Maybe things got out of your control. You had no real choice. Maybe you were a victim of the system. Maybe it was because all these people, places, and things were messing with you and pulled you down.

No, this is not the whole truth. Are you lying to yourself? Probably. No one wants to admit a serious mistake and come totally clean with it. Such work is hard, real hard.

This book will ask you to be honest with yourself—just yourself—not the cops, the prison staff, the probation officer, or even your wife or husband. Just read this with an open mind. There may be a simple reason for some, if not most, of the problems in your life.

When you ask yourself the questions in this workbook, answer them with the truth. Nobody is listening to your mind but you. Take some time to stop and look at your life. What do you have to lose? Just try.

Getting High and Doing Time: What's the Connection?

Do you have a problem getting high? Probably not. You know how to get high. You know good and well how to party. But has it become too important? Drinking, doing drugs, smoking crack, popping pills, shooting dope, or getting "fucked up" is real to you. It is how you live. It is your way of relaxing and "partying" with friends. It is your escape from the job, your boss, your husband or wife, or the crap in your life.

Think back a while in time to before you were on probation, parole, or locked up. Go even further back to when you first began to drink and do drugs. It made you feel good, real good. You probably remember well that first high or the first time you got drunk. Face it, the warm feeling or rush is good stuff. Yes, you want to do it over and over again. You want to chase that good feeling all the way down the road.

Why run after it again and again? Because it made everything okay. You felt strong, powerful, important, and a real part of the world. But soon, you saw you had to use, get high, get buzzed, or get stoned just to feel normal.

You even may have promised yourself that you never would get hooked like the others. You said things like, "I'm not a real alcoholic. I don't drink in the mornings." "I ain't no junkie, I don't use needles." "I don't need the stuff all the time." or "I just like to party once in a while." Sound familiar? You can "hold" your alcohol or drugs. Maybe that is something that even makes you feel good. How can you have a problem if you can hold booze or dope better than other people?

Keep thinking back in time to earlier in your drug use. It got worse. It went from good to bad. The stuff started to turn against you. Maybe you ended up getting high even when you did not want to, or after you swore to friends or family that this was it, "I'm finished with this stuff." You really meant it when you said it, too.

But living began to get really bad as you saw your promises broken. You tried hard. But damn—this stuff messed with you. You could not keep your word. You did the same things over and over again. You lost your control. You may not admit it to others, but you know deep inside. You lost some friends and your self-respect. You used drugs or alcohol even when you did not want to. It became the only way to feel "right." It had the power to make you do things against your will.

It finally got so bad that you were locked up or put on probation or parole. Look back over your history with the "system" (cops and courts) and answer this simple question: "If I wasn't messed up with drugs or alcohol in some way, would I be on probation, parole, or in prison?"

To further look at the link between your alcohol and other drug use and crime, answer these questions:

1. While under the influence of alcohol or drugs, or to get money to pay for stuff, I have been arrested for and/or convicted of the following: (Circle the letters of the items that apply to you.)

    A. Drunk driving, reckless driving, or driving without a license

    B. Public drunkenness, disorderly conduct, or vagrancy

    C. Selling drugs or possession of illegal narcotics

    D. Grand larceny or theft

    E. Any weapons offense

    F. Breaking and entering ("B and E"), larceny, burglary

    G. Any violent crime (assault, rape, homicide, manslaughter)

    H. Prostitution

    I. Forgery, passing bad checks, or passing bad script

    J. Other charges or offenses (write them out here):

    _____

    _____

    _____

2. How many times in your life have you been put in a detention center, jail, or prison? _____
   How many of these were because you were getting high? _____

3. How many times in your life have you been on probation, parole, or some other type of supervised community release? _____
   How many of these were caused by your alcohol or other drug use? _____

4. Have you ever violated your probation or parole (or any type of community corrections or supervision) because of your alcohol or other drug use (or because your probation officer said you were doing drugs)?

   ___ Yes   ___ No

5. Would your rap sheet or criminal record be different if you did not use drugs or alcohol?

   ___ Yes   ___ No. If yes, how?

   _____

   _____

6. If you see a link between getting high and your trouble with the law, can you put it in your own words? For example, you could say, "Every time I started drinking with the guys and getting back into my 'old habits,' I ended up getting busted again or having trouble with my wife." Or, you might say, "To get cocaine [or other drugs] I did some illegal shit, then got busted for it."

   _____

   _____

   _____

   _____

Understanding Addiction: Getting to the Bottom of It

OK, now you are starting to think about all this stuff. This is a good start. You are beginning to ask yourself some important questions. Maybe you even have decided to be honest (since no one is looking inside you).

You begin to see a connection between your drug and alcohol use and where you are this minute. Alcohol + drugs + you = rap sheet + arrests. And, remember that beer IS alcohol, too. Do not kid yourself. Drinking beer is drinking alcohol. But, let us go deeper into the basics. What is the matter with you? Why is all this shit coming down on you? See if Frank, Mary, Carol, or Stephen can help give you some answers. These are their own words.

I got addicted as a kid

I started drinking when I was 12 and started doing Meth ("crank", crystal meth, and so forth) when I was 13. By the time I was 16, I was hooked. Tried about every type of drug there is . . . I ate uppers, downers, and painkillers, freebased coke, shot heroin, dropped acid, smoked pot. I even took thorazine once, tryin' to catch a high.

For a while, getting loaded was the main thing for me. Couldn't go no time drug free or I'd get sick. To get money, I'd lie, steal, rob, con, cheat, scheme, rip off anybody. Even stole from my mom and cashed in savings bonds given to my son. Didn't give a shit about nothing or nobody. Shot a dude once over drugs. My addiction controlled me totally. Lost everything 'cause of it . . . family, jobs, money, self-respect, and my freedom.

— Frank, age 28

In my last DWI, I killed someone

I didn't really get hooked until I was in my 40s. I was a binge drinker and sometimes went months without drinking much. Then, I'd lose control and get drunk for a couple of days. I never had health problems or lost my job because of drinking and bounced back pretty well. The only problem I seemed to have was getting caught driving while I was loaded.

I always thought I was just unlucky and never thought about being an alcoholic. I went on drinking binges for about 10 more years. Then, during my last binge, I drove while drunk and smashed into another car, killing a teenager.

— Mary, age 53

I could handle heroin, then it handled me

My drug addiction started when I was 30. Before then, I never used drugs and only drank once in a while. A boyfriend turned me on to snorting heroin. I controlled my use for a couple of years and kept it hidden. Even after I got hooked, I managed to con others. My kids didn't know I used and neither did anyone at work except another addict.

As my habit got worse, I began to use before work or at lunchtime. But I seldom missed work. Drugs started controlling me more and more, becoming the most important thing in my life. I'm ashamed to say at one point they became more important than my kids. Can you imagine that? My life was totally out of control.

— Carol, age 40

I had everything—and lost it all

My parents gave me a good upbringing. I grew up in an upper-class family and had many advantages that others didn't have. During high school and college, I was good in just about everything I did, from my studies to sports. After graduating from college, I settled down and began raising my family. I worked as an accountant and made a very good living.

About 10 years ago, I snorted cocaine. I liked it but had a respect for it, so I limited how much I used . . . at least for a while. It's hard to say when, but after dabbling in it for a while, I really got hooked.

To support my very expensive habit, I stole money at work. Then, I started to sell cocaine. Following numerous problems at work I was fired. I ended up using all of my family's money to buy cocaine. After I got arrested a couple of times, my wife and kids left me. My wife said she had been through enough. I lost my job, my family, my dignity, and my freedom because of my love for cocaine. I'm paying the price for it now!

— Stephen, age 41

I rocked at all the "raves" until that night the agents busted down my door

Sure, I did it to myself really. I can't blame anyone. I should have known better all along, what with Dad and his drinking and drugging past. I thought I was different, though, smarter—you know. And I used to love going to the clubs—or raves, call them what you want—over the weekend. I'd be there every single weekend. I'd hang with friends, smoke, do a little X or sometimes some speed. But I was in control, man.

I knew what was happening to some of my friends. Not me, never. I started selling the stuff instead, almost to make sure I wouldn't go down that road. But, I did, anyway. Slowly. Started using more and more. Started making more and more excuses. Nobody could tell me anything, though. I thought I had it all under control, until the DEA knocked at my door. I'm doing federal time now, and they don't mess around—those sentencing guidelines keep you down a long, long time.

— Nick, age 23

Addiction: What is it?

Addiction is a disease. In many cases, it is a serious brain disease. What else would explain why someone would take a drug over and over again even though his or her life was coming apart?

The cases above show how addiction messes up lives in different ways. You can be addicted and not use every day . . . and not get high every time . . . and not always suffer serious problems in every area of your life.

Your addiction can start quickly and early in life, like Frank's. Or it can occur slowly over time like it did for Carol. It does not matter what type of childhood you had, you still can get addicted like Stephen did. On the surface, he had everything—a good home, a loving wife and children, a college education, and a well-paying job. But like many addicts, he lost it all.

Addiction affects all areas of health and life. It has to do with body, mind, and the environment. *Addiction is a sick habit that causes serious problems*.

The signs of this disease usually show first in your alcohol or drug use patterns. It also shows first in your behaviors, more so than in any medical problems. Because addiction is such a "sneaky" or "crazy" disease, *you will deny that it is a problem*. It may be obvious to others. But it tells you to say things like:

- I only use at raves.
- I don't use every day.
- I don't use in the morning.
- I don't use needles. I don't freebase.
- I only use as much as my friends.
- I have it under control—the problem is my job.
- Boozing or drugging don't cause me no problems.
- I don't get loaded every time I drink or take drugs.
- I only drink beer or smoke dope, no hard stuff.
- I work every day and support my family. How can I be hooked?
- I only snort coke. I don't smoke crack.
- I only "use" to relax now and again. I deserve it.

20

These are just a few ways you might deny your disease or illness. Because of this denial, *most people with addictions never get help*! Many of the lucky ones who get help do it at first to save a job or marriage. They get help only because someone else wants them to. They might say, "OK, I'll stop this shit for you, babe." In other words, they do it for someone else and not for themselves. That is OK for now. It is a good place to start.

What causes addiction?

No one knows for sure exactly why people get addicted. Doctors say some of us are just born with a tendency to develop addiction. It runs in families like other illnesses such as diabetes, cancer, or depression. Our family background stacks the deck against us, especially if we have an addicted parent.

People with addictions often react very differently to alcohol or other drugs than people who are not addicted. Their brains may be different as well. As a result of these physical factors, addicted people may not know when they have drunk too much alcohol.

Some addicts can drink quite a bit and not feel like they are drunk even when they are. They may build up a tolerance that leads to using a lot of stuff. They need more to get high. Or, they use more often just to keep the high. For other addicts, tolerance for the drug or alcohol goes down quite a bit and they cannot handle nearly as much stuff as before. They get loaded much quicker and on much less.

Think about these questions to help you see if you have some of these biological influences:

(1) Do you have a parent, grandparent, or other relative who is (or was) an alcoholic or drug addict?
(2) Are you able to "handle" large amounts of alcohol or drugs, amounts that would knock others for a loop?
(3) Once you start using, is it difficult to stop?

Psychological factors also play a part in this disease. These include your personality, how you deal with problems, and how you think about yourself and the world around you. Addicts often act without thinking. They are used to getting what they want right away. They like to escape reality and run from life. To cover up bad feelings inside, they drink or take other drugs. It settles them down. Because they feel different or unhappy about themselves, they use. Then they forget about the trouble they may encounter.

Social factors include access to drugs or alcohol and pressure from your family or friends. Maybe you lived in the middle of open-air drug markets where drugs were everywhere. Or maybe you lived with others who were addicted and talked you into "joining the crowd" and getting high.

Addiction results from a bunch of different things. Just try to remember this formula:

Body + thinking + emotions + personality + environment + alcohol/drugs
= ADDICTION

But the truth is, it really does not matter how or why you got addicted. What matters is what you do about your addiction.

Here's another way to think about causes and effects of this disease. Let's say five people jump off a 100-story building for various reasons. One jumps because he is angry. Another one is bored. One is depressed. Yet another is lonely. And the last one is looking for a dangerous rush. It does not matter why they jump because the end result will be the same. Death!

Think of addiction as the same type of thing. No matter how or why it happens, the results are the same—death or injury . . . for you, your family, or others. The idea here is not to search for reasons to explain it all away. The goal is to stop the hurt of addiction.

How Bad Is Your Addiction?
Do I Have the Disease?

Your first step toward help, and it is a difficult one, is to decide if you have the problem. Do I have the disease of addiction? Is my drinking or other drug use a problem? In this section, we have some questions to help you take a closer look at your alcohol or other drug use. Again, just be honest. That is all it takes.

1. On which of the following have you gotten high, drunk, stoned, or loaded? (Circle the items that apply to you.)

    *   Alcohol (Beer, Wine, or Liquor—all the same—all of it is alcohol)
    *   Over-the-counter Drugs (Robitussin, Nyquil, other cough suppressants, sleeping aids, or analgesics containing alcohol)
    *   Opiates (Heroin, Methadone, dilaudid, percodan, percocet, or other controlled prescriptions for pain management)
    *   Other depressants or downers (tranquilizers, and so forth)
    *   Cocaine, crack
    *   Methamphetamine ("crank," "ice," "speed," preludin, other uppers or stimulants)
    *   Club Drugs (MDMA, "ecstasy," Ketamine, "Roofies," and so forth)
    *   PCP or hallucinogens (LSD, STP, DMT, mushrooms, and so forth)
    *   Inhalants (glues, gasolines, solvents, nitrates, and so forth)
    *   Marijuana (pot or hash)

2. Which of these is your main drug of choice? (In other words, the one you usually end up using)? Write it out specifically.

   _____

3. Answer this question honestly: Are you always able to predict what will happen to you once you start using your drug of choice (or any of the drugs listed in question on #1)? Think of it this way: Are you always able to predict how much you might use or what might happen to you before you actually start using?

   ___ Yes, I can always predict what's up once I start drinking or drugging.

   ___ No, I cannot always predict what will happen to me once I start drinking or drugging.

4. Have you spent most of your extra money on alcohol or other drugs in the past year?

   ___ Yes

   ___ No

5. Which of these have you experienced as a result of your alcohol or other drug use? (Circle the * before the items that apply to you—the further down the list you have started to circle, the worse your problem probably is.)

   * Thinking too much about alcohol or other drugs (or obsessing about drug use)
   * Getting annoyed with your wife, husband, or partner's negative comments about your using
   * Having problems cutting down or stopping even when you wanted to
   * Having strong cravings or hunger for drugs or alcohol
   * Mixing drugs to boost their effects
   * Shooting drugs with needles even though you promised yourself you would not

* Using more alcohol or drugs than you intended (losing control)
* Having problems in your life (either family, work, friends, with money, and so forth)
* Doing stuff you promised you never would to get drugs or alcohol
* Quitting drugs and alcohol altogether but then starting again even though you really did not want to (relapsing)
* Feeling guilty about your drinking and drugging (having a feeling that your relationship to alcohol or other drugs is *different* than others)
* Feeling you can relate better to others (especially sexually) while high on your drug of choice
* Blacking out—not being able to remember what you did or said when using
* Being asked to check into or attend self-help group meetings, like NA, AA, or Rational Recovery
* Getting into trouble with the law (arrests, convictions, DWI's, reckless driving offenses, and so forth)
* Needing to use to start the day or needing to use every day
* Using to keep from getting sick or to stop withdrawal sickness
* Needing to use more stuff to get high (increased tolerance)
* Being unable to handle as much as before (decreased tolerance)
* Getting high at shooting galleries or crack houses
* Going to the hospital for detoxification or other accidents related to your drinking or drugging
* Death (hopefully, none of you circled this yet!)

6. Count the number of items or circumstances you circled above and write out the number here. _____

(Consider how far you went down the list. This is *progression*. It is what is likely to happen to most people if they keep on drinking and drugging. And, you can see what is at the very bottom of the list.)

7. Now, in your own words, describe how using alcohol or other drugs has affected your:

a. Physical or sexual health
    (for example, "I got hepatitis once from using—laid me up for a good long time.")

    _____

    _____

    _____

b. Mental health
    (for example, "I wake up feeling sad and anxious after a good 'party' weekend, then I promise myself, again, that I will not get high that way—I usually disappoint myself!")

    _____

    _____

    _____

c. Personality
    (for example, "My friend says that I always get nasty or change my attitude when I get drunk or high.")

    _____

    _____

    _____

d. Family or social relationships
    (for example, "I spend much less time with my family than I used to.")

    _____

    _____

    _____

e. Work/School
    (for example, "My job performance is worse now that I'm drinking more.")

    _____

    _____

    _____

f. Religious beliefs or practices
    (for example, "I used to go to church regularly before I started party-
    ing so much.")

    _____

    _____

    _____

g. Financial condition
    (for example, "Just bad, all bad, real bad—and mostly just because of
    my drinking and drugging, for sure.")

    _____

    _____

    _____

h. How many times have you been treated for your drug problem? _____
    What did you learn?

    _____

    _____

    _____

i. What are you willing to do to stop using and to start changing your
    life?

    _____

    _____

    _____

    _____

j. Are you courageous enough or willing enough to admit that you are an
    alcoholic or an addict and ask for help with your disease? Why? Why
    now?

    _____

    _____

    _____

    _____

Life-or-Death Choices: What You Can Do About Your Addiction

Life-or-death choices? You say "bullshit," that we are being too serious about all this stuff. Take an honest look at the facts! In the previous pages, you looked at your alcohol and drug problem. It is hard to run from the truth. *Your life has been screwed up real good by your addiction to booze or drugs.* You have a disease or illness, just like someone with cancer. Plain and simple. Now, what can you do about this?

First, accept the idea of progression. Your addiction is a disease that, if left alone, will get worse . . . even if you take "time out" from using while in the joint. There is no turning back once you have an addiction. Unless you make some positive changes, it will get worse. Probation will turn into parole. Short jail time becomes longer prison terms. Misdemeanors become felonies. Husbands and wives become ex-husbands and ex-wives.

Where will you end up if you do not start being honest about your disease? This is the idea of progression. Bad becomes worse. All because of a disease you can't control. A disease you did not cause.

Second, accept responsibility for doing something about your addiction (like "treatment" or "recovery"). You are not to blame for becoming addicted, just like the cancer victim is not responsible for having cancer, or the diabetic for having diabetes. But they have a duty to help themselves get better. We expect them to take their medicine, to eat the right food, to see their doctors, and to follow any other treatment plans. We do not want them to die. And we do not blame them for being sick with their disease either.

This process is the same for the addict. You are in serious need of a good recovery plan to get help for your disease. You are a sick person, not a bad person.

Your choices may be hard to make, but at least they are basic. To change yourself and "arrest" your disease, you must be willing to:

- Ask for some help.
- Listen to others who have gotten help for their disease and are in recovery.

If you do not want to change, and you will not accept responsibility for getting help for your addiction, it will get worse. Maybe you will be able to catch it later on, before it really nails you to the wall. But then again, maybe you won't.

Remember Judy in the introduction to this booklet? Her drug of choice was crank (speed, crystal) and then ice (smokable methamphetamine). She kept saying she was going to "kick this shit" on her own. She liked to see herself as real strong since she made it on the streets for years. At first, she blamed her probation officer for being the problem. She did not want to see her drug use as a life-and-death situation. Judy did not want to get help. Check this out, though. Here Judy is later on after changing her mind:

I ended up doing 18 more months. Yeah, my PO eventually violated me. My habit got real bad and I couldn't find no clean urines to give up. I was losing weight, looking real bad, and not giving a shit about nothing but where I could cop some crank or ice.

Social services came and took my daughter, man. God, this shit really does make you act crazy. Deep down, I thought when I did my time and hit the streets again it wasn't going to be no different. What the hell was the use?

But I started going to NA (Narcotics Anonymous) meetings in the joint. I checked those people out real good at first. Listened closely to their rap. And dig this. The shit started sinkin' in. I don't know what exactly happened, but I realized I was one sick MF to be using all that dope and not care about nothing. Or nobody. Not even my daughter.

When I got out of the joint, I kept going to NA meetings and got a sponsor. I got into a drug program even though I stayed clean in prison. Go to a group every week where we rap about staying clean and changing ourselves.

I let go of some of my guilt and shit about the past. Even started seeing hope for me! My attitude's changed a lot. Got rid of my deep anger. Cut loose my junkie friends. A lot of the stuff I used to cut up in the NA program is helping me now. As bad as my addiction was, recovery seems to be working for me.

Judy did not think it was going to be any different when she got out of prison. Then, she went to some NA meetings. As the days went by, she was able to admit that she was addicted. She saw it progressing from bad to worse. Judy had to stop using if she was to have a chance at life. She liked herself enough to do something. She took the first step by asking for help. She even went to a treatment program after she had been clean from drugs in prison for a year and a half. If Judy can do it, you can, too!

Getting Out of the Addiction Trap: Recovery Works If You Give It a Chance

By now, you know you have some hard choices to make. You can keep getting high. You can let your addiction run your life. You can put your addiction on hold until you finish your time in jail or on parole or probation. You can then start getting high again. You can even get high while on parole or probation and try to get over on your PO.

Or, you can make choices that will help you out of the addiction trap. No matter how bad your addiction is, and no matter what price you've paid for it, you can turn things around now. Especially if you choose to ask for help and start to work a recovery program.

Even if you are not using now, or you have not used for a while, even if you have been straight for sometime, or if you are locked up, recovery can begin. Right now. Recovery can begin if you give it an honest try. Think of it this way: If you give recovery a shot and you don't like it, you always can go back to using drugs or alcohol, like before.

Just stopping alcohol or drug use is not recovery. It is a good start, but only a start. You also must change! Change things like how you think about yourself and the world, who you hang out with, and how you live. Change yourself. It is that simple and that difficult.

You might think, "Isn't giving up booze or dope enough? I mean, after all, that's a pretty big change for me. What the hell else do you expect from me?" You are right. Giving up the stuff is a big change for you. But that alone will not cut it.

Listen to Lou's story about how he changed after he quit using.

I'm 37 years old and a grateful recovering addict. I spent about five of the last ten years in jails and prisons. Passed bad checks, robbed, assaulted people, and a few other things. Most of this resulted from being loaded or needing money to get drugs.

After my first stint, I had to go to treatment as a condition of my parole. I did OK for a long time, but not because I wanted to. Because I had to. Anyways, my addiction got out of control again and I began to rip people off, sell drugs, and do other crimes.

The first time I got caught with a hot urine, my PO cut me a break. He really tried to get me to work my recovery program and get my shit together instead of putting me back in jail. Well, to make a long story short, later he caught me in a couple of lies and with another hot urine. So, he popped me and put my ass back in jail for violating my parole.

I resented him for a long time and blamed him for my troubles. It's a typical con game we cons play. Avoid responsibility by blaming others. We're the poor victims. What a crock!

For the first couple of months in jail, I continued to get shit to get high on. Thought I was a hotshot because I got drugs smuggled in to me. After finishing my time, and luckily not getting busted while in jail, I had some charges in another state and got more time. So, I was transferred to another prison.

I stayed clean for a couple months. Went to some NA meetings and started to learn about addiction and recovery. I heard this guy talk about overcoming his serious personality problems and addiction. He sounded a lot like me. So, I got my public defender to get me in a treatment program after my time was up! I'd been clean almost a year but still felt treatment could help me.

I had a few days between prison and treatment, so what did I do? Got high a couple times. But I still went to treatment. Finished a 28-day rehab program, then eight months in a TC [therapeutic community]. It took me a couple of months to develop a serious desire to stay clean and change. I've changed some of my character defects or personality flaws, like my short fuse, selfishness, and tendency to lie and con others. Don't get me wrong, it wasn't easy. I'm still working at it, but I'm changing. I'm getting rid of what I call my "conning mentality" and have a better sense of right and wrong.

Also changed my relationships. I started taking an interest in others like my parents and sisters, instead of using them for money, a place to stay, or to bail me out of trouble. Faced their anger and distrust of me when I sat down to make amends to them for the problems I caused. They really lit in to me, but I deserved it. Things are OK now between us. I don't feel so guilty now for all the stuff I put them through.

Probably my biggest change was how I relate to women. Before, I mainly used them for sex, drugs, and money. Always could find someone to take care of me and let me move in. Went from woman to woman, dumping them when I got bored or didn't have any more use for them. Well, that kind of selfishness is changing, too. I'm going slow and actually went a couple of months without seeing any woman because I needed to focus on my recovery.

One other change I wanted to mention is my beliefs and my use of this idea I got in NA called "Higher Power." I never was one for church, religion, or God. But I go to church now and pray to my "Higher Power." I started developing faith.

Since I've been clean a while, I'm able to reach out and help other addicts. But only because I've been helped and I chose recovery over addiction. Counseling and working the Twelve Step program of NA have really helped me. I still have things I need to change. But I'm on my way. And still clean. And not locked up!

Lou's case shows how his addiction was a big factor in his criminal lifestyle. Like many others, he was "forced" into treatment. He did OK for a while before going back (relapsing) to drug use and doing his thing again.

Accept the need for recovery: Motivation for change

Most people in trouble with alcohol or other drugs do not wake up all of a sudden one morning and decide to go for help. No! It sometimes takes years of the disease progressing. Sometimes it takes a traumatic or really ugly incident to motivate the person into treatment or into asking for help. That is okay. Sometimes it takes the criminal justice system to start the wheels turning in someone's mind about whether or not they may have a problem.

Addicts who do not honestly want help initially, but get involved in treatment only to save their butts from getting in trouble, still can gain from it. But help is available only if they come around to accept the need for recovery. Once in treatment, you may find it can help you, and that you can change your life.

Lou's interest in recovery did not come easy. He had a rough time. At first, he was not even sure he wanted or needed to stay clean. He paid a high price for his first relapse when he lost his freedom again. But Lou did not give up. He gave it another chance.

He chose to go to a long-term treatment program after he had been clean from drugs for a couple of months in prison. Lou put himself at risk for "violation" by getting high between release on parole and starting his treatment program. Lucky for him, he still decided to try a treatment program. This was his third time in professional treatment! It is never too late to try! Some people are more stubborn than others. Some put up with more and more pain before they finally get help.

Let's look again at some of the things Lou was able to do in his recovery.

- He got clean and stayed clean from drugs and booze by attending a lot of NA meetings, getting a "sponsor," and getting into a professional treatment program.
- He accepted his personality flaws or defects that needed changing.
- He changed some of these flaws. He stopped getting pissed off and always lashing out at others. He started being more honest with himself and was less self-centered or selfish.
- He changed his "conning mentality" and stopped using and ripping off others, getting a better sense of right and wrong.
- He made his family relationships better—less one-sided and more two-way—and made some apologies to them for the hurt he caused.
- He stopped "using" women only to meet his selfish needs.
- He worked on his spirituality and began believing in a power greater than himself.

This is quite a list of successes for Lou, especially given his long rap sheet and his lack of concern for others. How did he do all this? It was simple. He "worked" a recovery program. Lou went to counseling for a long time. Even though he has been clean for several years now, Lou still goes to NA meetings. He talks often with his NA sponsor. And he practices the principles of recovery in his life. He "lives" the program. Lou now helps other suffering addicts. He chairs an NA meeting in a local jail.

Lou will be the first to tell you that life is not always good or fair. Things do not always go well. But he will also tell you that things are a lot better now. With the help of NA's "living tools" and counseling, he made his life better. He has choices today that he never thought he had.

Recovery: Yours for the taking

We could give you hundreds of other success stories like Lou's. Inmates who complete a treatment program while in prison are much less likely to return after their release. Studies have proven that recovery can work. It can help you stay clean—and out of prison.

We also could tell many stories of failure and of addicts returning to prison. The difference between success and failure lies in your attitudes and the choices you make. There are a lot of people who will help you recover. Just remember the bottom line—only you can decide if and what you will change. Recovery is yours for the taking.

If you decide not to recover today, you can change your mind later. Many addicts choose not to get help for their addiction, only to later change their minds. The point is this: Recovery will remain a choice to make.

If you keep putting recovery off, you are at higher risk to mess up again. Like Judy, who was a three-time loser and came back for a minimum ten-year sentence after robbing somebody to get money to buy dope. Or Frank, who left prison and went back to hanging out with his old buddies on the street. He got right back into doing some bad shit, then shot and killed someone. Frank's a lifer now. Judy and Frank, both addicts, saw no reason to get help for their addiction after getting out of prison. Each went right back to using. It was only a matter of time before they got busted and sent back.

Many professional and self-help programs exist to help alcoholics and drug addicts get and stay clean or sober. If you are doing time, check out the programs available where you are. Ask about rap groups, counseling, AA and NA meetings, or other types of programs.

You still may need help when you get out. Since there are so many types of programs out there, you should see somebody at an alcohol or drug treatment clinic. Then, you will have a better idea about your treatment options. Your probation officer will also be able to help you in this area. Remember: By admitting your problem and asking for help, you give yourself the chance to get out of the addiction trap.

The First Step: Using AA, NA, and Other Self-help Programs to Change Yourself

Many people like Lou and Judy have found a way to deal with their addiction. They have found a way to stay clean. They have made new friends. They have found a direction in their life. They have found a reason for living. They have done all this by taking things one day at a time. And, they have done all this without booze or drugs. Sound impossible? Not at all.

Some of you know exactly what we are talking about here. Yes, Alcoholics Anonymous (AA) and Narcotics Anonymous (NA). AA and NA are groups of recovering alcoholics and drug addicts who meet regularly to learn how to get and stay clean. They also learn new ways of coping without using alcohol or other drugs. Your chances of making it get much better when you stay in AA or NA.

The first step is to be open about what AA and NA are. Get rid of negative or bad attitudes about them. AA and NA members are not a bunch of skid-row drunks, druggies, or junk heads sitting around in circles and talking about religious mumbo jumbo.

Not true at all! They are people like you and me. They are people who suffer from the disease of addiction. They are people whose lives have become messed up because of addiction. They come from all walks of life—mechanics, steel workers, truckers, lawyers, ministers, parole agents, teachers, laborers, mothers, grandfathers, doctors, nurses, electricians, secretaries, waitresses, and ex-cons.

Just as addiction does not care what your social class or job status is, neither does AA or NA. If you want to be a member, all you have to want is to stop drinking or taking drugs. Even a little or half-hearted desire is enough to be a part of AA/NA. Your desire to quit may change later.

AA/NA is not a religious program. It is not at all like church. They do not force you to believe a certain way about God, or even that you must believe in God at all. It is more a "spiritual" program. By this we mean they encourage people to start looking outside of themselves for help with their addiction. This is where they talk about a "Higher Power" (HP for short). Your HP can be your God if you want, or it can be anything else you want—your AA/NA group, your sponsor, just as long as it is not you!

AA/NA will never tell you what you must believe. You must want it and take the first step in reaching out for some help. There are no leaders or people in charge. Money is not involved. No one gets paid for leading AA or NA meetings. It costs no money to attend meetings or to become a member of a group.

Now, if you are dead set against NA or AA, that is okay. Do not give up. You should at least try AA or NA for at least several meetings (most recommend at least ninety meetings, in fact) before you make up your mind to go elsewhere. Just make sure. And then, by all means, try other types of self-help group meetings out there, like Rational Recovery, church-based groups, men's/women's rap groups in some communities, or even professional groups centered around stopping the insanity of drug or alcohol addiction. Addiction is a BIG community problem. Lots of people and professionals have become good at helping, and they are out there if you just look. The best people to ask about some of these other groups would be your community leaders, probation or parole officers, and church leaders. They will know and be willing to point you in the right direction.

Tips for using self-help programs

Here are some tips for using these self-help programs for your recovery from the disease of addiction. Most of these tips are geared toward the traditional NA or AA meeting. That is okay. They also apply to other self-help groups, like Cocaine Anonymous, Pills Anonymous, and even non-twelve step groups like Rational Recovery. The key is to find a group of people who have been through what you have been through, who understand what you have had to put up with, and who can help lead and guide you through the recovery process.

1. If you are in prison now, find out if there are meetings going on inside. Start attending if there are. Do not wait until you hit the streets!

2. Ask the people in the meeting for AA/NA reading materials (pamphlets, the "Big Book" of AA, the "12 and 12," or the "Basic Text" of NA). You can also check the prison library for recovery materials or ask that they order some.

3. During AA/NA discussion meetings, talk and share your stuff with others in the group. Ask questions about things you want to know about the program and recovery. Listen to people who are clean and sober.

4. Be real about it. You will not like every meeting or every person you meet. Take what you like and leave the rest behind.

5. Before you get out of prison, ask the people in the prison meeting to get you a meeting list. Make attending meetings a high priority in your life. If staying sober and clean becomes your number one thing, other things in your life will work out over time.

Once you are out of jail, or if you never went to jail and are on probation instead, here are some more suggestions:

1. Find a "sponsor" to help with the Twelve Step program. A sponsor is someone who has been in recovery and has a lot of clean time in the program. A sponsor can teach you about recovery, help you find good meetings, and help you meet sober or clean people. A sponsor will be a friend who knows the real "no-bull" you. And your sponsor knows when you are being honest about recovery.

2. Make sure you get a sponsor who is the same sex as you. This helps to avoid emotional or sexual problems that can mess up your recovery.

3. Ask for help. AA/NA members feel good when they are helping someone else stay straight and work the program. This is how they "give back" what they "got" from the program. They want to help, but they cannot read your mind.

4. In early sobriety or clean time, attend lots of meetings. Listen. Give them a chance to work for you. Keep an open mind and try a couple dozen or more meetings before you even think about judging them. Attend "ninety meetings in ninety days," if possible. This way, you place sobriety and being clean as your number-one goal.

5. Pick and choose your meetings. Not all are the same. They are different. You may want to search around for meetings with people to whom you feel you can relate. There are morning, noon, evening, and weekend meetings. If you have unusual work hours, find meetings that fit your schedule.

6. Find a "home group" or a meeting that you can go to regularly each week. Ask to make coffee, clean up, or put away chairs. This can help you meet people. You will begin to feel part of the group.

7. Stay around after the meetings to talk with people. Get some phone numbers. Go out for coffee after the meetings.

8. Try not to set yourself up to feel different just because you have done time or are on probation or parole. So have many of the other members at some point in their lives. No matter what the differences in backgrounds, you all have the disease of addiction in common.

9. Try different types of meetings. There are "speaker's" meetings, "open," "closed," "discussion," "step" meetings, and so forth. Look for "beginner" meetings when you first start the program.

10. There are only two times when you need to go to meetings: (1) when you don't feel like going and (2) when you do. You usually will feel better afterwards, even when you have to drag yourself there.

11. If you like what a person says, talk with him or her after the meeting. Look for feelings, thoughts, and experiences that are like yours. You will hear, see, and feel the hope in the meetings. Stick with the winners.

12. Take your recovery one day at a time. Have you ever been sober or clean for twenty-four hours before? Sure. And you can do it again, just for the day. And remember, it is the first drink or drug that will get you in trouble. Do not take the first one. Pick up the phone and call your sponsor or an AA/NA friend instead.

13. Use the "Higher Power" idea. Put your faith in God or something or someone outside of yourself. The idea is to recover with the help of others — not on your own, alone.

14. Learn about the "Twelve Steps" and use them. A sponsor can be very helpful in teaching you about these steps.

15. Use AA/NA to buy time until an inpatient or residential program bed is ready for you. It is too bad, but because so many people are trying to get help these days, there is just not enough bed space in treatment centers. Be aware of this and do not take it personally. Don't use this as an excuse to pick up again. Instead, use the program, go to meetings, reach out, and buy yourself some valuable time until a bed is available.

Keep in mind that even if you tried AA or NA in the past and you did not like it or did not feel it helped you, it can be different this time. Just give yourself another chance. For some people it takes years of going in and out of AA/NA before they "get it." Just be willing to try. That is all you need. The rest usually will fall into place.

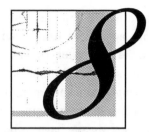

Relapse Prevention: How to Stay Clean After You Get Clean

My relapse took me by surprise

I was clean from dope for over six years. I did good in my recovery and even helped get a lot of NA meetings started in my hometown. My life turned around through the fellowship of NA.

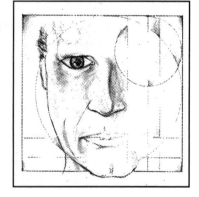

Then, I got a script for pain pills following dental surgery. My body had a very strong reaction to the pills. My addiction came back to life! The pills made me feel good. I was reminded of all the times I got high.

Very quickly, my thinking got screwed up. Soon, I cut down on, then stopped, going to my NA meetings. Conned my sponsor and NAs into believing I wasn't feeling well and needed time to rest from surgery. It wasn't long before I was buying pills on the street. One thing led to the next, and soon I was passing bad scripts. Within two months of my relapse, I totally lost control and was using every day.

My wife and kids were real upset with me. My boss couldn't depend on me at work. l can't believe how I went from doing so well in recovery to getting hooked again. Then, to doing crimes to get my drugs. And messing up my job and hurting my family.

— Stan, age 39

Getting sober or clean is one thing. Staying sober or clean is quite another. "Relapse," or going out again and using, can happen any time in recovery. Stan's case shows how he was taken by complete surprise. He started using again after years of being straight. Both he and his family paid a heavy price.

When recovery (staying clean and changing yourself) is the number one thing for you, relapse is less likely to happen. But it still can happen, as it did with Stan. That is why you always have to be on your toes. Do not get over-confident. And do not take your recovery for granted, like there ain't nothing to do, like it's a piece of cake!

The first year in recovery, and especially the first couple of months, is the time you are most likely to use drugs or alcohol again. This is because your body is getting used to being without alcohol or other drugs. Your addictive thinking is still there, alive and well. People, places, and things remind you of using. They tempt you and tease you. Desires to use jump out at you!

If you stayed clean while in jail, you might go back to using when you first get out. If you believe your addiction is "cured" because you were clean while in jail, you are setting yourself up for a relapse. Many addicts put their addiction on hold while inside. And, then, as soon as they hit the street, because they feel better and believe they have control, they start getting high again. The addiction cycle starts all over again. The pain very quickly returns.

Your best way to prevent a relapse is to:

- "Work" a recovery program (AA, NA, and/or counseling).
- Understand relapse as an ongoing process. It has warning signs or clues that show before you pick up again.
- Make a plan of action to deal with your relapse risk factors.

Working a recovery program

Alcoholics and drug addicts who work a recovery program do much better than those who do not. They stay sober or clean longer and improve their lives.

Because addiction is such a terrible and deadly disease, many people stay in recovery programs for years and years. Some even make it a lifelong process. There are many alcoholics who have not had a drink in years, and many drug addicts who have not used drugs in years who still go to AA or NA meetings. For many, it is a new and healthy way of life.

Your best way to prevent a relapse is to be active in working a program of recovery. "Working" a program means trying out the principles of recovery all the time. It means going to AA, NA, or other self-help meetings. And it means knowing when you may be headed for a relapse. By making recovery from addiction your number one goal, you raise your chances of success. Carol's experience shows this point.

My recovery is my number-one priority

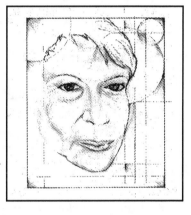

My drug use caused me and my family a lot of heartache. It was a big factor in my going to jail. When I got out of jail, I told myself that I would do every thing I had to in order to stay clean. Being away from my kids had been so hard. It made me feel sad and depressed, and very guilty.

Even though I haven't taken any drugs in over five years, I still go to NA meetings and work my recovery program because I know that relapse still can happen to me. I practice the Twelve Step program of recovery, talk with NA friends and my sponsor regularly, and sponsor people in NA. No matter how busy my life gets, I make sure my recovery from drug addiction remains my number-one priority.

I've had my share of problems and setbacks during the past five years. But I know that I can take care of them only if I continue to stay clean. I'm a grateful recovering addict and feel a whole lot better about myself and my life.

— Carol, age 40

Relapse is a "process"

Relapse is a process and not an event. It starts before you actually use alcohol or other drugs. Relapse clues or warning signs show before your use. They show in changes in your attitudes, thoughts, moods, and/or behaviors (how you act).

Sometimes relapse clues are obvious and you know you are headed for trouble. You do things such as:

- Go to parties where people are getting high
- Seek out old friends you used to party with
- Go to bars or clubs to drink soda, shoot pool, hang out, or dance
- Cut down or stop AA/NA meetings or counseling without a good reason for this
- Substitute one drug for another or "limit" how much you use (no cocaine or heroin, just a few drinks; no booze, just some herb now and then)

Or you think such things as:

- I am really okay now and my addiction is under control
- It was not all that bad when I was using
- Being straight is a drag, and I need some action
- I can control this stuff; I'll just have a few drinks or toots tonight
- I don't need AA/NA like the rest of those people; I'm different

Other times the *clues are sneaky* and do not seem to be linked to a possible relapse. They seem totally unrelated. You:

- Become moody, depressed, or real uptight
- Feel upset and pissed off but do not know why
- Get angry and resentful for no real reason
- Quit caring about yourself or your recovery
- Get cocky and think your habit is licked
- Become sneaky or dishonest in other areas of your life
- End up with people or in places you know you should not be

Sometimes the warning signs last a very long time. The sooner you know your signs, the quicker you can take positive action.

The following case shows how Ron was in a relapse process before he ever picked up a drug. By being alert and working his program, Ron stopped himself from using. But it sure was a close call!

I caught myself just in time

I had my own business and made a very good living. I sometimes got high on liquor or pot. Then, I started using cocaine and freebase. I became obsessed and greedy for base and would do anything to support my habit. I spent my family's savings, sold our stocks and bonds, cashed in my insurance policies, and took a second mortgage out on our house. Within a short time, I was broke and my life was in shambles.

I got arrested following a minor accident in which they found cocaine and a gun in my car—on the front seat! The judge ordered me to treatment and put me on probation. This actually saved my life, as it forced me to stop using. I slowly put the pieces of my life back together.

After doing well for nine months, I started thinking about drugs. I missed the "high times." I told myself I would stay away from freebasing and only snort coke once in a while.

It's like I convinced myself I wasn't really an addict anymore. I also felt edgy and restless and wasn't sure why. Something wasn't quite right but I didn't know what. Yet, I acted like everything was alright when I was with NA friends. I avoided them, then began skipping my meetings.

A few weeks later, I called my old dealer. On the drive over to cop some coke, I kept telling myself I was crazy. I began doubting my ability to control my use if I started again. I thought about the negative shit my addiction did to me and my family.

After stopping for gas, I called a friend in NA and told him what I was doing. He was cool about it. Told me to come to his house right away. We could rap about stuff. We talked for over three hours and he helped me get hold of myself.

I leaned on my friend, NA sponsor, and other NAs to help me through the next couple of days. My desire to use left and my addictive thinking also changed. I was able to avoid a relapse because I used my support network and the tools of recovery. I waited until I was pretty close, but I kept myself straight. It was my first big test in recovery. But I made it.

— Ron, age 27

If you were in recovery before, take the time to learn from your past relapse(s). Identify the warning signs that were there before you went back to using. Learn from your past mistakes.

Many addicts know when their warning signs are present, but they just do not care. Others do not have a "plan" to take positive action *now*. Remember, addiction will tell you not to give a damn about your recovery. Your disease wants you to get high, no matter what. That's why you have to learn how to respond to warning signs and have a plan to fight the "I don't give a damn" or "I want to get high" attitude.

Making a plan of action

A relapse prevention plan is simply an *action plan*. It is a list of things to do as a way to deal with your problems or "high-risk" situations. Risky situations in recovery are those times you used alcohol or other drugs in the past. If you used when you felt lonely, bored, angry, or upset in the past, you are at risk to use when you are lonely, bored, angry, or upset in the future. Learn new ways to deal with these emotions. If you are with a partner who abuses alcohol or drugs, this is a relapse risk for you.

The most common relapse risk factors are the following:

- Having negative emotions (anger, boredom, depression, loneliness, guilt and shame, or feeling empty, like nothing matters to you in life)
- Having memories from your past that still hurt real bad
- Having negative thoughts or "stinking thinking"
- Returning to a denial of your addiction
- Feeling pressures from others to use alcohol or other drugs
- Hanging with old friends who still get loaded; or going to old places, bars, or clubs where others are using or getting high
- Having strong cravings or urges to get high
- Feeling like you want to celebrate the "old way"
- Having mental health problems or other kinds of addiction that do not get treated (depression, gambling, and so forth)
- Doing things without thinking them through first (for example, quitting a job suddenly, hitting someone you love, and so forth)

- Making big changes in your life before talking with other sober or clean friends
- Not making a serious promise to work your recovery program. This is done by not putting forth your best efforts at changing yourself or your lifestyle (flying by the seat of your pants and only doing enough to get by; not going to AA or NA meetings; not getting a sponsor, and so forth).
- Not putting a stop to "getting over" (for example, lying, scheming, conning, or using others)
- Taking certain medications for medical or psychiatric problems. Your body does not know the difference between drugs used to get high and drugs used for medical problems.

If you need medicine for a medical or psychiatric problem, make sure you tell your doctor about your addiction. This way, he or she can make sure the correct medicine is used. The doctor also can watch how you react to the medicine. Also, be sure to let your sponsor know.

Working with a counselor and/or sponsor is one of the best ways to honestly face your risk factors for relapse. In the previous section, you saw how Lou's recovery process came about. To stay clean, he had to change his conning mentality, his temper, his way of lashing out at others, his problem relating to women, and his lack of meaning in life. These are some of the things that Lou needed to change so he could reduce the chances of a relapse happening.

Stopping relapses

Relapse is a reality. No one is totally protected from it. Because relapse can take you by surprise, you really need to think about it and know what to do if you find yourself getting high again.

We are not saying this will happen, but are pointing out that you should be prepared. Think back to the case of Stan at the start of this section. His relapse took him by surprise. He paid dearly for it because he was not prepared.

Since you are involved in the criminal justice system, the price you pay for a relapse can be extra high. You have added pressures that other addicts do not have. A relapse for you could mean a violation of your parole and getting busted again.

On the other hand, we know of cases where addicts have been helped by their POs when they have gone back out and used. If you are really trying to help yourself, and not trying to get over, your parole or probation officer just may help you.

The earlier you catch yourself when you start using again, the better able you may be to stop it. John, an alcoholic, was sober for more than two years. One day he took a drink without thinking first. He soon realized he had made a mistake and stopped. He talked about this with his sponsor and AA group. He kept working his recovery and did not use again. John is doing well again.

Fred, on the other hand, had quite a different experience. He had been sober for more than eight years. While away on vacation with his wife, he had some physical pains and anxiety. He thought a few shots of whiskey would help "settle his nerves." As soon as he took the first drink, however, Fred's thirst for booze came back. He lost all control and went on a drinking binge for six weeks. He was very upset with himself. His family was upset as well. Fred could not stop his relapse and went back to a rehab program to get back on the sober track.

No one can tell if using once or twice (called a lapse) will end in a full-blown relapse where addiction controls you again. A good recovery plan could include one or more of the following to stop a lapse:

- Calling your sponsor
- Going to an AA/NA meeting
- Asking others for help
- Telling yourself to stop using now
- Talking to your PO or corrections counselor
- Reminding yourself of the problems your addiction caused
- Reminding yourself of the benefits of sobriety
- Asking your higher power for inner strength to stop using
- Keeping busy or getting involved in a project or activity to occupy your time

Thinking and planning ahead keeps you from sitting back helplessly and allowing your addiction take over again.

Notes on my relapse prevention plan

Stated another way, relapse prevention is dealing with your overall self and making positive changes in several different areas of your life. For each of the areas listed below, take some time to write out what your specific plan will be to avoid relapse. Consider talking to your sponsor, probation officer, or counselor before finally deciding what to write. You may list several options under each heading:

I. My personality (for example, "I will stop beating myself up so much for doing 'bad' things while intoxicated.")

_____
_____
_____
_____

II. My ways of coping with problems and life (for example, "I will call my sponsor before getting into an argument with my wife or husband.")

_____
_____
_____

III. My addictive thinking and negative attitudes (for example, "I will try to keep things simple and focus on staying away from that drink or drug 'one day at a time.'")

_____
_____
_____
_____

IV. My use of time (for example, "I'm going to start spending my Friday evenings at the 24th St. Serenity Club meeting, instead of at the other night clubs.")

_____
_____
_____
_____

Your Family and Recovery

Stan talks about how his family was left behind

Over the years, my addiction caused a lot of problems. One of the things I feel real bad about is how I hurt my wife and three kids. I was so busy taking care of my need for dope that I ignored my kids. I really wasn't much of a father. My kids tried so hard to get attention and love from me. I was just too damn much into my addiction to see how much they needed me.

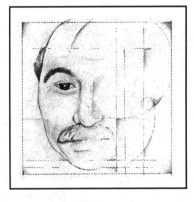

My wife stood by me through thick and thin. All I did was put her through hell! When I got busted and sent to jail, they got another bum rap. They write me and visit me, but I feel pretty damn rotten for what I did to them. I'm worried about my oldest son. My wife tells me he doesn't listen. She thinks he's getting high. He just doesn't seem to care. It's like he's repeating my pattern. I feel pretty helpless to do anything. My daughter cries every time she comes to visit me. It makes me feel so guilty what I put them through. Believe me, everyone in my family suffered from my addiction.

Maria says she is just like her mom

When I was younger, I told myself I'd never be like my mom. She was an alcoholic and just couldn't take very good care of us. My dad was heartbroken and tried his best to keep the family together. If it wasn't for him, I don't know what we would've done. I promised him I'd never be like Mom. Wouldn't you know I got into drugs and booze when I was fourteen. In a couple of years I became hooked. I did some of the same things my mother did.

What bothers me the most was how I disappointed my father. I was hurt by my mother's problems, so I can imagine how he feels about what I've done with my life. It wasn't bad enough his wife was an alcoholic. Now his daughter is one, too. I'm going to do everything I can to turn myself around before it's too late. My mom never got help. At least, I have a chance.

Eugene says it is so hard to forget

My dad drank every weekend when I was growing up. When he wasn't drinking, he was a pretty nice guy. The drunker he got, however, the more of an SOB he became. He got mean and violent towards my mother, me, and my brothers. A couple of times when he was drunk, he made passes at two of my sisters. They're still upset over this.

Dad lost a lot of jobs because of his drinking. We were always broke. He often spent our food and rent money on booze. We got evicted twice. We spent a lot of years on and off welfare and living in public housing. I can remember having our gas and lights cut off a couple of times. There were even times when we did not have any food in the house.

Me and my three brothers got in trouble all the time. Mom covered up a lot so dad didn't know about our problems. Two of us quit school. My brother straightened himself up, got a good job, and settled down. I continued to be wild and out of control and ended up in jail.

Dad never writes or visits me. He just doesn't care. I have so much anger built up against him, sometimes I think I'll explode. It's just too hard to forget what he put me and the family through. I ain't blaming him for my problems, but maybe things would've been different if he showed he cared about us.

You can see in these cases that addiction hurts families, too. Stan put his wife and kids through hell. They are still paying for it while he sits in jail. Sadly, his oldest son is headed for trouble now.

Maria got addicted even though she told herself she would not be like her alcoholic mother. This shows how a son or daughter can become addicted even though they feel that they never will be like their addicted parent.

Eugene and all his family were exposed to a variety of problems directly related to his father's addiction. These included violence, money problems, emotional abuse, and sexual abuse. Eugene still feels very pissed off at his father, even though it has been years since he has lived at home. This intense anger has been part of many of his troubles. If he doesn't learn to let go and heal from this, Eugene will go on having serious problems in his life.

Addiction can mess up the entire family. In families where a parent is addicted, there are higher rates of divorce, violence, and other kinds of serious problems.

Addiction can affect the un-addicted (straight) family members' physical or mental health, attitudes, values and beliefs, relationships, and self-esteem. Any family member—husband, wife, brother or sister, children of all ages, or other relatives and friends—can experience the bad effects of a loved one's addiction.

In some cases, the impact is strong. The effects may be long-lasting. In fact, the effects may still be felt even if the addicted parent is no longer alive or part of one's life.

The sad thing is how innocent children are hurt by a parent's addiction. These kids are more likely to develop drug or alcohol, mental health, school, or behavior problems. There is a good chance they will feel bad about themselves and not be happy. Even when they do not show problems and seem OK on the outside, a youngster or teenager can carry the scars of his or her parent's addiction.

Think of your own experience. Did you grow up in a family in which your parent was an alcoholic or a drug addict? If you did, take some time to answer the following questions.

1. How did it feel to grow up with an addicted parent?

   _____
   _____
   _____
   _____
   _____

2. What was it like for you on a day-to-day basis? What are some of the things that you remember the most?

   _____
   _____
   _____
   _____
   _____

3. What impact did it have on your life as you were growing up?

   _____
   _____
   _____
   _____
   _____

4. How are you affected today by what you went through back then?

   _____
   _____
   _____
   _____

5. Is there any connection between what you went through with your addicted parent and the behaviors that led to your trouble with the law? If yes, what is the connection?

   _____
   _____
   _____
   _____
   _____

Effect of your alcohol/drug use on your family

1. How did your use of alcohol or other drugs, and how you acted, affect your family? (Circle all the items that apply)

   • I caused a lot of suffering in my family.

   • Some family members may never forgive me for things I've done.

   • I neglected or avoided family responsibilities.

   • I caused serious money problems.

   • My alcohol/drug use often ruined family holidays or special occasions.

   • I stole from family members.

   • I never repaid money that I borrowed.

   • I lied or conned my family to get money for chemicals or to cover up my problem.

   • My use of alcohol/drugs led to a separation or divorce.

   • My use led to one or more of my children being taken away from me.

   • One or more of my kids is abusing alcohol or drugs.

   • One or more of my kids is having trouble with the law.

2. How else was your family affected by your addiction? (Include positive effects, such as they got closer with each other.)

   _____
   _____
   _____
   _____
   _____

3. If you have children, how were they affected by your addiction?

   _____
   _____
   _____
   _____
   _____

4. Do any of your children have an alcohol or drug problem?

___ Yes ___ No

5. Are any of your children in trouble with the law?

___ Yes ___ No

How you can help your family now

If you and your family have not gone separate ways, there are some things you can do that may help. Do not be surprised if they resist your suggestions at first. They may see the addiction as your problem only. Even if they covered up and lied for you, or experienced mental suffering because of what you put them through, they may say they were not bothered by it. They may believe that since you are doing time and have not used in a while, there is no reason for them to get help. Here are our suggestions on what you can do to help your family:

1. *Take care of your addiction problem.* Get the treatment you need and stay off alcohol or other drugs. If you do not take care of your problem, do not expect to help your family very much.

2. *Talk openly about your addiction.* It is time to stop sweeping it under the rug and acting like it is not a major problem. It will not go away by not talking about it. At some point, you and your family need to sit and have a face-to-face talk about how the addiction affected everyone.

3. *Say you are sorry (make amends) for the pain you caused your family.* The best amends or change you can make is to not use drugs or alcohol one day at a time. You can also make amends by being honest and admitting the things you did to hurt your family during the times you used alcohol or drugs.

   Making amends will succeed only if you are sincere in your efforts to apologize and undo some of the damage caused by your addiction. Remember, your actions speak louder than your words. Do not say you are sorry if you do not mean it.

4. *Ask your family to learn the facts about addiction.* They can do this by reading and by attending Alateen, Al-Anon, Nar-Anon, or other family support group meetings or educational sessions at a treatment center. The more they understand, the better they can help your efforts at recovery as well as help themselves.

5. *Ask your family to attend support groups.* These include Alatots for young kids, Alateen for teenagers, and Al-Anon and Nar-Anon for adults. There also are special programs for parents and adult children of alcoholics/drug addicts, such as Adult Children of Alcoholics. Support groups help people to get involved in their own recovery and make some personal changes. As a result, they often feel hope for the future, get over their emotional pain, and become healthier. Plus, they are less likely to "sabotage" or mess up your recovery.

6. *Ask your family to get counseling, if needed.* If any members of your family are having serious problems that they cannot work out on their own, or with the help of a support group like Al-Anon or Nar-Anon, they should seek professional counseling.

You must be patient with your family. Recovery can be a painful and difficult process for them, too. It takes some people years to get over the negative stuff. Living with an addicted family member is very hard. Try to respect your family. Do not put down what it might have been like for them.

My plan for improving family relationships

Consider what you have just read and start thinking about ways of improving your own family relationships. For each heading that applies, write out what your plan is for improving your relationship—what you (not them!) can do to make things better:

Children (for example, "I plan to spend more time with my kids on Sundays and weekends."):

_____

_____

_____

Intimate partner, wife, husband, or lover:

_____

_____

_____

Extended family (parents, grandparents, or others):

_____

_____

_____

Parole and Probation
Officers: Working with Them

Getting along with your PO can be easier than you think. What does it take?

- Be honest about recovery.
- Attend NA/AA meetings and other types of treatment.
- Work hard at staying clean and changing yourself.
- Be willing to ask for help, one day at a time.

If you do all these things, there won't be any major issues with your probation or parole officer.

What will happen if you stay away from alcohol, drugs, slippery places, and people you know will try and play with your head? You will make it on parole or probation. It is that easy—that simple. Why is that? More often than not, your problem has been fooling yourself about alcohol or drugs. When you pay attention to getting treatment for your disease, your PO has nothing on you! Nothing!

Okay. It is not always quite this easy, we admit. Sometimes you get a PO who may not understand addiction. Or in the beginning, you may have trouble staying straight for any length of time. You may relapse and start using again. What do you do? Do you tell your PO or hope he or she does not find out? What if you have to give up urine samples for the PO? How about missed appointments or not getting slips signed that you attended AA/NA meetings or counseling sessions?

The key is this: *If you make your recovery from addiction your number one priority, even more than job or family, other things are more likely to fall into* *place. If recovery becomes a low priority, it just will not work.* There are no shortcuts, quick fixes, or easy ways out. Staying straight one day at a time must be the most important thing.

Here are a few ideas that others have found helpful in working with, instead of against, their POs.

1. *Keep all appointments.* You want to gain the respect and trust of your agent or officer. One of the things they hate the most is clients who do not report as directed. It makes you look as though you have something to hide. It also shows that you are not being responsible in carrying out your obligations. Call if you need to change your appointment. This is responsible behavior.

2. *Follow the PO's directions.* Do this even if you do not agree with them or think they are full of crap. You are the one who will lose in the end if you do not. Besides, they will not be around forever in your life. If you are serious about getting better from your addiction, use the "program" (AA or NA) and talk with your sponsor about it. This will help you "blow off steam."

3. *Go to your AA/NA or other self-help group meetings.* Practice the principles of recovery in your daily life. You will have little or no problems with your PO if you truly are "working" your recovery program and not using stuff or trying to get over.

4. *Be honest.* You can lie once or twice, but in the end, it will hurt you more than anyone else. POs are used to dealing with lies, and most are pretty good at catching lies and liars over time. If you keep lying, eventually you will screw up and get caught. Then, it will be hard to get your PO's trust again.

5. *Go to counseling if you feel you need it, or if your PO or the court recommends it.* More than likely, your PO will not listen to excuses as to why you think you are different and do not need counseling. You might be surprised at how this can help you, if you allow it to.

6. *Try not to get mad at your PO when he or she asks for urine samples.* The PO is only doing a job and carrying out the court's or prison's orders. He or she may also be doing you a favor. Having to give urines can help you stay away from that first drink or drug.

   Many addicts have told us this "check" was helpful, especially in the beginning of recovery when they felt real tempted to get high. It is not unusual for drug treatment programs to take urine samples, even when patients are not on probation or parole. People who object most to this are the ones trying to get over on the system.

7. *Admit relapses.* Do not hide this information. Talk about it and get it out in the open. Get your POs support by being honest about it. Many POs really respect this. Remember, they are used to clients lying and trying to BS them. Be different and tell the truth.

8. *Ask for help if you are relapsing.* Maybe you need a different type of recovery program. Your PO can help you get into different types of residential or outpatient programs. If you are sincere in your efforts to ask for help, most POs will be interested in seeing you get better.

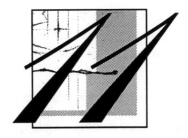

Mental Health Problems:
Getting the Help You Need

Our main goal in writing this book was to help you deal with your alcohol or other drug problem. However, we want to make you aware of the importance of seeking help if you have a serious depression, bipolar problem, severe anxiety, psychotic tendencies, or personality disorder. A serious mental health disorder (also called a psychiatric disorder or mental disorder) refers to a condition in which your symptoms cause you personal suffering, interfere with your relationships and ability to get along with people, or cause you problems in your life.

These disorders are very common—about one in four adults in our country will experience symptoms of a mental health problem at some point in his or her life. These problems are much higher among people with alcohol or drug abuse—almost four out of ten people with an alcohol problem, and more than five in ten people with a drug problem, have an additional mental health problem. These rates are even higher among people who have trouble with the law.

If you have any of the mental health problems discussed on the next few pages, you should talk with someone you trust to help you figure out what kind of help you may need. It can be anyone like your PO, a relative, friend, doctor or other health care professional, counselor, priest, minister or rabbi, or some other adult with whom you feel comfortable. Tell them what is bothering you and ask them to assist you in finding the correct help for your mental health problem. Or, you can call a mental health clinic or a professional who provides treatment in a private practice such as a psychiatrist, psychologist, social worker, pastoral counselor, therapist, or counselor. If you see a private practice therapist, make sure he or she is licensed to provide the kind of treatment you are seeking.

Help for mental health problems may come in a variety of forms. It may include counseling or therapy, medications, attending a self-help program, and/or participating in some type of special educational or vocational program.

Mental health problems (psychiatric disorders)

Many people with alcohol or drug problems have psychiatric disorders or behavior problems that, if not treated, cause personal suffering and interfere with their life and emotional well being. It is not unusual to feel "different," guilty, shameful, or stigmatized if you have a mental health problem.

There are many different psychiatric disorders, and each has a complex set of symptoms, related behaviors, and negative effects. Many people have more than one of these, in addition to their substance abuse problem.

Our list below only highlights a few of the more common mental health problems found among people who have drug or alcohol abuse or dependency. Keep in mind that these disorders are very difficult to diagnose in people who continue to use alcohol or drugs. An accurate diagnosis usually requires a period of time of being sober from alcohol or drugs. It also is a good idea to get a physical examination since some medical problems can contribute to psychiatric symptoms.

Review the following list of problems and note the ones that apply to you. Discuss your results or any concerns you have about your mental health with a trusted person to help you figure out if you should get professional help. If you are not sure you need help, you always can meet with a qualified mental health professional once or more to seek advice on whether you need counseling or other treatment. These descriptions are not meant for you to diagnose yourself, because you cannot. However, if these descriptions seem to fit you, then you should see a professional for an evaluation to determine if a disorder exists that could be treated.

1. *Major depression* that persists for two weeks or longer and causes you personal distress and/or difficulty with any aspect of your life. By serious depression, we mean deep feelings of sadness or hopelessness along with any of these symptoms:

    *   loss of interest in your daily activities
    *   poor appetite, gaining or losing weight without trying to

- sleeping too much or having trouble falling or staying asleep at night
- poor concentration and trouble thinking clearly
- trouble making decisions or remembering things
- feeling irritable
- feeling worthless or helpless
- thinking about or planning to take your own life

Episodes of clinical depression may last months or longer without effective treatment. While some people only experience one episode of depression during their lives, others experience multiple episodes over time, a condition referred to as *recurrent depression.* Other people experience many depressive symptoms most of the time for several years or longer, a chronic condition referred to as *dysthymia.*

2. *Bipolar disorder* (previously known as manic-depressive illness) in which *mania or an elevated mood* is present that persists for several days or longer. This mania is like feeling high or very hyper without being on drugs. An elevated mood may come along with any of these symptoms:

- decreased need for sleep or going one or more days without sleep
- talking more than usual
- racing thoughts
- trouble sticking with one idea at a time
- being distracted easily from what you are doing
- a significant increase in activities or jumping from one activity to the next
- getting involved in activities with a high potential for problems (for example, sex with multiple partners, spending sprees, and so forth).

3. *Serious anxiety* that causes you distress or difficulty in your life or being with other people. Anxiety may show in physical symptoms such as

- racing heart
- feeling dizzy
- sweating

- shaking
- nausea or stomach pains

Anxiety may show in thoughts such as fear of going crazy, losing control, or dying. Anxiety also may show in your *phobias*, which involve behaviors such as avoiding people or groups or situations you fear such as flying, riding in elevators, or closed spaces.

4. *Obsessions and compulsions* that cause you a lot of personal distress or cause difficulty in your daily life. *Obsessions* are persistent thoughts or images that keep popping into your head. They are much stronger than normal worries that we all have from time to time. Obsessions can relate to bodily secretions, dirt or germs, bugs, diseases, collecting things, sex, keeping things in order, religion, aggression, or many other things. *Compulsions* are behaviors you repeat over and over, usually to make your obsessions go away. These can show up in repeatedly checking things (doors, windows, locks), repeating words or phrases, cleaning, washing your hands or showering excessively, hoarding or saving things, repeating or counting things over and over, or putting things in order, that would be considered excessive by others. People with more serious types of obsessions and compulsions are often looked upon by others as strange, weird, or eccentric.

5. *Psychotic disorders such as schizophrenia.* Psychotic symptoms include having confused or disordered thoughts, being out of touch with reality, talking in ways that do not make sense to others, or talking about bizarre things or acting in a bizarre manner. These symptoms usually interfere to a large degree in your life. Examples of symptoms include: hallucinations such as hearing voices others cannot hear; having delusions or false beliefs that you are somebody famous, have special powers, or that others are out to control your thoughts or harm you; paranoia or a belief that others are out to get you; and having trouble knowing the difference between reality and fantasy. In many cases, psychotic disorders involve low motivation, low energy, depression, and a tendency to isolate yourself from other people.

6. *Attention deficit and hyperactivity disorders.* Attention-deficit refers to a pattern of inattentive, hyperactive or impulsive behavior that has been

present at least six months or more and that interferes with your development. Examples of *inattention* include:

- you do not pay attention
- you make careless mistakes
- you cannot stay focused on school, work, or other activities
- you have trouble listening
- you do not follow through with instructions or obligations
- you cannot get organized and structure your time or life
- you avoid tasks that require your attention over a period of time
- you often lose things
- you are easily distracted or you are forgetful

Examples of *hyperactivity* include:

- you fidget or squirm
- you get up often because you cannot sit still
- you feel restless
- you have trouble playing or participating in activities quietly
- you feel like you are "driven by a motor" or always have to be "on the go"
- you talk excessively

Examples of *impulsive behavior* includes

- blurting out things to others
- having trouble waiting your turn
- interrupting others or butting into their conversations

7. *Antisocial personality disorder.* This involves a pattern of behavior in which you violate the rights of other people or break the law. It starts during your teenage years and can show up in any of the following behaviors:

- failing to abide by the law
- deceiving others by lying or conning them
- being aggressive by threatening, intimidating, fighting, or hurting others

- acting impulsively by not thinking things through or planning ahead
- showing disregard for your safety and that of others
- engaging in a pattern of irresponsible behavior such as not paying your bills or taking care of your work or other responsibilities
- displaying a lack of guilt or remorse when you hurt, mistreat, or steal from someone else

People with this disorder often had problems during their teenage years such as destroying property, lying, stealing, breaking into stores or peoples' homes, and violating rules such as staying out late, running away from home, or skipping school. Almost 85 percent of people with this personality disorder have problems with alcohol or drug abuse, too.

Suicidal thoughts and feelings

Suicidal thoughts are common with many psychiatric disorders as well as with alcohol or drug abuse. You may wish you never woke up or were dead. Or, in more serious cases, you think you would like to take your own life and you begin to think of ways of doing this. *If you feel suicidal, you should take this very seriously and seek help immediately, especially if you have a plan, are worried you will act on this plan, or you have actually made an attempt! If you have a past history of attempting suicide, or are currently using alcohol or other drugs, your risk of suicide increases significantly.* Keep in mind that suicide is a permanent solution to a temporary problem.

Intense anger or problems with violence

If you feel intense anger or rage inside of you, or if you act out in violent ways toward other people, you should ask for help immediately from a counselor or therapist. Counseling can help you learn to let go of your anger in safe and healthy ways. It also can help you know when to keep a lid on your anger and not let it out. Counseling can teach you ways to deal with your problems and conflicts in healthy ways so that you do notlashout or act violently. You also can learn how to deal with anger directed towards you from other people so that you do not let them trigger your anger or rage.

If you have a recent history of child abuse, domestic violence, or assaulting other people, you should make sure you get help with this problem. Both therapy and medications such as mood stabilizers can help, depending on the specific nature of your problem.

Living with a violent, mentally ill, or addicted person

If you currently live with a friend or family member who has a serious psychiatric problem, an addiction to alcohol or drugs, or a problem with violence, you should make sure you have a *safety plan* so that you do not get hurt. This may mean going to a shelter or a neighbor's or relative's house when this person gets out of control. Counseling can help in many ways such as learning to deal with your feelings, learning how to deal with your family member(s) who has one or more of these problems, and figuring out what you can and cannot do to help your family member. Support groups are often an excellent source of help.

Serious problems in relationships

While most people have problems in relationships from time to time, some have more serious and persistent problems. These include: (1) relationships in which another person wants you to break the law or pressures you to do things you do not think you should do; (2) a high maintenance relationships where you cannot seem to satisfy the other person no matter what you do (this can be a friend or romantic partner); (3) a demanding relationship where the other person wants a lot more from you than you can give; (4) an abusive relationship in which the other person constantly puts you down or physically hurts you; and (5) a relationship with another person who often uses you, does not listen to you or seem to care about your interests or needs, and makes you feel like things are one-sided.

How to help yourself

Here is a summary of ways that you can help yourself if you have any of these problems.

1. Acknowledge your mental health problem. Do not deny it, pretend it does not exist, or wish that it simply would go away. Mental health problems do not usually go away for a long time until they are treated.

2. Do not be a victim and passively accept that there is not anything you can do. Of course you cannot change another person such as a father with a drug addiction, a violent brother, or a mother who is very depressed. What you can do, however, is take care of yourself and learn to manage your own life. This can involve learning to deal differently with other people.

3. Seek advice about what your options are. Talk to a trusted person about your problem and get advice on whether you should seek some type of professional treatment. If you are advised by a professional to attend a special program (for example, for domestic violence, anger management, managing depression, or coping with substance abuse and psychiatric disorders combined), trust their advise. Do not take the easy way out.

4. Follow-through with getting help. It is not enough to admit you have a problem and need help. You have to actually follow through and take advantage of the help available. Keep your appointments. If you get into therapy or counseling, go prepared to discuss your problems and how you can change. If your disorder requires the use of medications, take these only as prescribed. Do not stop them on your own, take more than you are prescribed, and do not mix these with alcohol or other drugs.

5. Attend support groups for mental health problems. Programs such as Dual Recovery Anonymous (DRA) use the twelve-step program of AA for dual disorders of psychiatric illness and substance abuse. Some mental health support groups such as Recovery, Inc. or Emotions Anonymous are "generic" and available for any type of mental health disorder. Other programs are for specific types of problems such as depression, bipolar illness, anxiety disorders, or schizophrenia.

6. See problems for what they are—problems to be solved rather than a reason to give up, feel victimized, or give you a reason to mess up. Many people in trouble with the law have had tough breaks or a rough childhood, but these are not valid excuses to keep messing up. You have to choose to be responsible for your life, your happiness, and act responsibly at home and on the job.

How counseling or therapy can help you

Mental health therapy or counseling sessions can help you in several ways. First, you can learn more about your disorder and the best treatment for it. Second, you can discuss your thoughts, feelings, and problems contributing to, and resulting from your mental health disorder. Third, you can learn about yourself and why you do the things you do. Fourth, you can learn ways to manage your disorder and make positive changes in yourself. And fifth, treatment can help you reduce the chances of a future psychiatric relapse by helping you spot relapse signs early and taking action.

How to get the most from your counseling or therapy

Your sessions are most effective if you attend them on time, go with specific problems or concerns to discuss, set goals to work toward, identify steps you can take to reach your goals, ask for feedback on your progress, regularly evaluate how your treatment is going, and you can discuss any negative feelings you have toward your counselor or therapist. Do not be shy if you feel upset with your therapist. Let him or her know. Do not run away from these feelings. Also, do not be quick to get rid of your therapist if he or she tells you some things that you did not like to hear or if you have a disagreement.

When medications are needed

Medications for psychiatric disorders are used when your mood, anxiety, and psychotic symptoms are severe, cause you suffering, or significantly interfere with your ability to function. The purpose of medications are twofold: to reduce or eliminate major symptoms of your disorder; and to reduce the odds of your having a future episode. Some people take psychiatric medicine for several months and stop after they have been symptom free for several months or longer. Others who have chronic conditions such as recurrent depression, bipolar disorder, schizophrenia, or some of the anxiety disorders, take medications on an ongoing basis. While one medication may be enough to treat a disorder, sometimes a second or third one is needed. Most psychiatric medications are not addicting and will not interfere with your recovery from addiction. However, medications such as tranquilizers are very addicting, so you need to be cautious about these medicines.

You should not stop medications on your own without discussing the reasons with a doctor or with your counselor, as this often leads to a psychiatric relapse. Also, try to avoid asking for more medications or a new medicine every time your symptoms flare up or you feel bad. Sometimes, you have to learn to live with some symptoms some of the time. Finally, medications cannot do anything to change bad relationships or unhappy life circumstances. You have to work on these issues in therapy. Medicines help by reducing psychiatric symptoms and putting you in the position to use your therapy more effectively.

Final Thoughts and Action Reminders

Many people in trouble with the law have a serious problem with alcoholism and/or drug addiction. In many cases, addiction is a big part of this trouble.

We have seen many people in prisons, jails, or on parole or probation turn things around in their lives because they got involved in a recovery program. Recovery programs—AA/NA and/or professional treatment—have helped many get off and stay off alcohol and other drugs. Many people have changed themselves and their lifestyles as well. It is no secret that recovery works—if you do your part.

In this book, we asked you to start facing the truth about your addiction. By even taking the time to read this book, you have shown that you are ready and willing to begin recovery.

Action reminders

These are the main points of this book:

- Addiction is a serious disease, but it is very treatable. Day in and day out, addicts get help, even those who felt hopeless at one time or another.
- Problems with alcohol or other drugs increase the chances of your getting into trouble with the law or having to do time.
- Recovery is your responsibility. Others can help you, but you have to be the one to stay clean.
- Recovery is not only quitting drugs or alcohol but changing yourself.
- Go to AA and NA meetings, get a sponsor, and work the Twelve Steps.

- Go to a rehab program if you need it, even after you have been clean while in jail or prison.
- Get professional counseling if you need it. Many addicts have emotional or personal problems in addition to addiction and benefit from one-to-one or group therapy sessions.
- Do not pick up a drink or drug just for today; take your recovery "one day at a time."
- Addiction affects families, too. They can benefit from education, counseling, and/or self-help programs such as Al-Anon or Nar-Anon.
- Recovery can bring good things to you and your family.
- Do not give up if you lapse or relapse. Keep trying. Learn from your mistakes.
- Work with your probation or parole officer.

We want to end with a passage from Alcoholics Anonymous, called the "Big Book" of AA. This book promises great things if a commitment to sobriety and staying straight is made.

If we are painstaking about this phase of our development, we will be amazed before we are halfway through. We are going to know a new freedom and a new happiness. We will not regret the past nor wish to shut the door on it. We will comprehend the word serenity *and we will know peace. No matter how far down the scale we have gone, we will see how our experience can benefit others. That feeling of uselessness and self-pity will disappear. We will lose interest in selfish things and gain interest in our fellows. Self-seeking will slip away. Our whole attitude and outlook upon life will change. Fear of people and of economic insecurity will leave us. We will intuitively know how to handle situations which used to baffle us . . .*

The Twelve Steps of AA/NA

The steps for NA are almost identical; just substitute the word "addiction" for alcohol in step #1 and "addicts" for alcoholics in step #12.

1. We admitted we were powerless over alcohol—that our lives had become unmanageable.

2. Came to believe that a Power greater than ourselves could restore us to sanity.

3. Made a decision to turn our will and our lives over to the care of God as we understood Him.

4. Made a searching and fearless moral inventory of ourselves.

5. Admitted to God, to ourselves, and to another human being the exact nature of our wrongs.

6. Were entirely ready to have God remove all these defects of character.

7. Humbly asked Him to remove our shortcomings.

8. Made a list of all persons we had harmed and became willing to make amends to them all.

9. Made direct amends to such people wherever possible, except when to do so would injure them or others.

10. Continued to take personal inventory, and when we were wrong, promptly admitted it.

11. Sought through prayer and meditation to improve our conscious contact with God as we understood Him, praying only for knowledge of His will for us and the power to carry that out.

12. Having had a spiritual awakening as the result of these steps, we tried to carry this message to alcoholics and to practice these principles in all our affairs.

The Twelve Steps of AA are reprinted with permission of Alcoholics Anonymous World Services, Inc. Permission to reprint the steps does not mean that AA has reviewed or approved the content of this publication nor that AA agrees with the views expressed herein. AA is a program of recovery from alcoholism. Use of the steps in connection with programs which are patterned after AA but which address other problems does not imply otherwise.

The Serenity Prayer

Many persons who are looking for help with their addiction problem find the following prayer very helpful. If the word "God" bothers you, use "Higher Power," or just leave it out altogether. The important point is that you are asking for help. You are admitting you might need some help outside yourself to stop your addiction. You cannot change the fact you have the disease of addiction. You can change what you do about it, with help from the outside (whether it be God, your AA/NA group, your sponsor). Try it and think about the words:

God, grant me the serenity to accept the things I cannot change, the courage to change the things I can, and the wisdom to know the difference.

Suggested Readings

Alcoholics Anonymous. *Alcoholics Anonymous* (Big Book), 3rd edition. New York: Alcoholics Anonymous World Services, Inc., 1976.

_____. *Living Sober: Some Methods AA Members Have Used for Not Drinking.* New York: Alcoholics Anonymous World Services, Inc., 1975.

_____. 1984. *Twelve Steps and Twelve Traditions.* New York: Alcoholics Anonymous World Services, Inc. (Also known as the "12 and 12")

Daley, Dennis. 1988. *Surviving Addiction: A Guide for Alcoholics,* Drug Addicts, and Their Families. New York: Gardner Press.

_____. *Relapse Prevention Workbook: For Alcoholics and Drug Dependent Persons.* 1986. Holmes Beach, Florida: Learning Publications.

Hazelden Educational Materials. 1987. Staying Clean: Living without Drugs. Center City, Minnesota: Hazelden Educational Materials.

Narcotics Anonymous. 1983. *Narcotics Anonymous* (Basic Text). Sun Valley, California: Narcotics Anonymous World Services.

Self-help Organizations

Alcoholics Anonymous World Services, Inc.
P.O. Box 459
Grand Central Station
New York, NY 10163

Al-Anon Family Groups (for your families)
P.O. Box 862
Midtown Station
New York, NY 10018
212-302-7240

Black Women in Recovery
P.O. Box 19003
Lansing, MI 48901
517-543-0084

Cocaine Anonymous
P.O. Box 3357
Phoenix, AZ 85067
602-277-7991

Emotions Anonymous International
P.O. Box 4245
St. Paul, MN 55104

Nar-Anon, Inc. (for your families)
P.O. Box 2562
Palos Verdes, CA 90274
310-547-5800

Narcotics Anonymous World Services
P.O. Box 9999
Van Nuys, CA 91409

Oxford House, Inc. (Transitional housing opportunities)
9312 Colesville Rd.
Silver Spring, MD 20901
301-587-2916

Pill Addicts Anonymous
P.O. Box 278
Reading, PA 19603
215-372-1128

Rational Recovery Systems (RR)
P.O. Box 800
Lotus, CA 95651
916-621-4374

Publishers of Recovery Materials

Hazelden Educational Materials
P.O. Box 176
Center City, Minnesota 55012

Learning Publications, Inc.
P.O. Box 1326
Holmes Beach, Florida 34218

About the Authors

Edward M. Read, LCSW, MAC, is a supervisor for the U.S. Probation Office in Washington, D.C., and has worked in the field of corrections for more than twenty years. He is a graduate of Columbia University School of Social Work with prior experience in the federal prison system, county probation and parole, and with the Administrative Office of the U.S. Courts (the Federal Corrections and Supervision Division) as a drug program and policy specialist. He also has served as a Federal Judicial Center faculty member for new officer orientation and addictions consultation. Mr. Read has written extensively in the area of addictions for a variety of professional trade publications and is the author of the joint Hazelden/ACA book entitled *Partners in Change: The 12-Step Referral Handbook for Probation, Parole and Community Corrections.*

Dennis C. Daley, Ph.D., is Associate Professor of Psychiatry and Chief of Drug and Alcohol Services at the University of Pittsburgh Medical Center, Western Psychiatric Institute and Clinic. Dr. Daley has been involved in substance abuse treatment and research for more than two decades. He has provided training for the Pennsylvania Board of Probation and Parole on chemical dependency problems. He has authored or coauthored many books, recovery guides, and educational videos on addiction and mental health problems. His practical recovery materials are used in many treatment programs throughout the United States and other countries.

Notes

Notes

Notes